# Crafty Kids: Make Your Own Craft Supplies

## Stories and Recipes for Crafting Fun

### By Rhetta Akamatsu

For Claudia, William, and Sebastian, the best
grandkids in the world!

## PREFACE

## WHY MAKE YOUR OWN CRAFT SUPPLIES?

1. It's cheaper.
2. It's fun.
3. You control the ingredients so that you always know what's in everything.
4. Letting the children help you make the supplies is educational and a great cross-curriculum experience..
5. You will encourage creativity in the children and in yourself.
6. Did I mention it's cheaper, and it's fun?

Read on  for some fun stories and to discover how you can create wonderful craft supplies for you classroom, daycare, Sunday School, or home out of the most amazing ingredients!

## 1 . Clay You Can Eat

Claudia was playing with clay in the
classroom. It smelled so good!
"Wouldn't it be fun," she thought, "if we could
make things out of this clay
and then eat it?"
She told the teacher, Ms.Rydell, how much she
wanted to eat the clay, and her teacher
laughed.

"Claudia," she said, "You can't eat this clay. But
tomorrow, I will bring in some
ingredients and we will make some clay you
can eat."

This is the recipe Ms. Rydell brought in the
next day:

### Edible Play Dough

1 cup peanut butter
1 cup honey
2 cups of powdered milk

In class, Ms. Rydell measured the ingredients
carefully into a big bowl as the children
watched. Then, she invited them to take turns
washing their hands and then kneading the
dough with their hands. It was sticky and fun,
and they all laughed and had a good time.
Then, Ms. Rydell gave each child some of the

dough clay, and they had fun making flowers, snakes, and figures out of the clay. When they were all finished, they ate their clay creations for snacks1

Claudia loved the clay she could eat, and so did the other children in the classroom!

"Next time," said their teacher, "we'll try to make some clay with brown sugar and peanut butter with granola. And maybe I'll find some more dough clays we can eat to experiment with."

You, your mom, or your teacher, can find more play dough you can make, including some you can eat, in the back of the book.

## 2. Playing Make-Believe

Claudia, William and Sebastian were bored.
They couldn't think of anything to do.
"Let's make believe," said Sebastian. "I'll be a
tiger, and William can be..
"A bear!" cried William. "And Claudia can be...
"A Princess, of course," said Claudia, who was
always a princess, after all.

"But we need makeup," Sebastian sighed.

"Oh, that's ok," the children's mommy
explained, "We can make makeup ourselves!"

Mommy went into the bathroom and brought
out a jar of cold cream. (Claudia wondered
why it
called that, but when she asked, Mommy
didn't know.) Mommy mixed the cold cream
with a little cold water and some cornstarch
and found some food coloring left from
coloring eggs at Easter. She put a little bit into
different paper bowls, and added different
food coloring to each bowl.

"There!," she said. "Now you can be whatever
you want to be!"

Claudia and William and Sebastian had a great time being tigers and bears, Princesses, and space aliens, all afternoon, and when they were tired, Mommy just used the cold cream and all the makeup came right off!

This is the recipe the children's mommy used:

**Face Paint**

(For each color)

1 tsp. cornstarch
1/2 tso, cold cream
1/2 tsp cold water
Food coloring

You and Mommy can find lots more recipes for painting and coloring at the back of the book.

### 3. A Sticky Situation

Sebastian's mom gave him a notebook, and she said he could do whatever he wanted with it. Sebastian decided to make a book about motorcycles like the one his Daddy had. He found lots of pictures and cut them out, but there was no glue!
Luckily, Sebastian's grandma knew how to make glue. She got some flour from the cupboard, and poured a cup and a half of it into a pan. She turned the stove on low, and slowly heated the flour and water, stirring it as

she did, until it was as thick as paste. Then she turned it off, and let it cool, and gave Sebastian a plastic knife to spread it with. It worked! Sebastian's motorcycle book was a big hit with everybody.

Here is Sebastian's grandma's recipe for paste;

**PASTE**

3 C. water
1 1/2 C. flour
Oil of peppermint (optional)

Stir flour into cold water. Cook over low heat until the
mixture thickens to a creamy paste. Add more water if the paste gets too thick.

(This paste also works great for papier mache'. The peppermint is just to make it smell good.)

Find lots more sticky recipes at the back of the book!

## 4. GOOD OL' GOO

William really loved to make a mess. He liked sticky stuff like clay and dough and he liked to get it everywhere!

But William's Mom was so fond of messes as William.

"Let's make something that is sticky and feels messy, but won't stick to everything," said Mom. "Let's make Flubber!"

William , Sebastian and Claudia giggled.

"Flubber! What a funny word!"

And after they made the Flubber, they found it was just as much fun to play with!

(Flubber is a kind of putty, that sticks to itself but not to other things.)

Here's the recipe they used:

## Flubber

Metamucil
Water

Place a teaspoon of Metamucil in a jar with 8-10 ounces of water.
Shake vigorously for about 60 seconds
Pour contents into a medium cereal bowl.
Place the bowl in microwave at full power for 4-5 minutes It will start to " rise" just like bread dough...but in fast speed.
Turn off the microwave when bubbles are just about to overflow the bowl
 Let it cool slightly and repeat- the more often you repeat this the more rubbery flubber will become (five times should do it )
Pour onto a plate or cookie sheet. Keep children away at this point! Teacher should stir until it cools.  . When finished it's cool and clammy but not sticky. Flubber will last for several months if tightly sealed or refrigerated.

If your Mom or teacher doesn't have Metamucil handy, you can find another recipe that uses liquid starch in the back.

## 4.  BUBBLE STUFF

The children's grandmother, Star, was just
crazy about bubbles. In the Spring, she loved to
play outside with the children  blowing lots
and lots of giant bubbles, letting them float in
the air. Grandmama Star taught William,
Sebastian, and Claudia how to make great,
long-lasting bubbles. This is what she did:

**Crazy Bubbles**

Put 1 quart of water in a shallow tub. Stir in
1/2 cup sugar until it
dissolves. Add 1/2 cup dishwashing liquid
&stir again. Have kids dip in
a slotted kitchen spoon or fly swatter, & swing
it in the air.

You can also cut both ends out of an empty
frozen juice can. Dip one end in the
bubbles  & blow through the other. Makes
huge bubbles!
Note: For color, add food coloring. You can
also buy glycerin at the drug store and add a
few tablespoons to make bubbles last longer.

In the back of the book, there are even more
easy recipes for making bubbles.

## 5. A Fourth of July Parade

It was the 4th of July and Claudia, William and Sebastian had gone downtown with their father to watch the big parade. Now, they wanted to have a parade of their own! They wanted things to wave in the air, like the people leading the bands had.

"I know how to make streamers!" exclaimed Claudia. "My teacher told me how!"

Claudia knew that there were several empty paper towel rolls in the kitchen cabinet, saved just for crafting. She ran and got them. She covered the table with newspaper, and grabbed her box of art supplies from her room.

"First, we glue construction paper around our paper towel rolls," she told the boys. Claudia chose purple, William chose blue, and Sebastian chose red.

"Now, we decorate them," Claudia instructed. They had a great time coloring designs on their tubes and then sprinkling them with glitter.

There was some crepe paper in the art box, so Claudia showed the boys how to cut it into strips and glue it to the top of their tubes.

Now they took their beautiful streamers and treated the grown-ups to a wonderful parade all around the back yard at Grandpa's house!

For some ideas for things to do for other holidays, like a great cauldron for Halloween, a cute gift for Mom for Mother's Day, and more, look in the back of the book!

### 6.  Claudia's New Room

Claudia had a new room in Daddy's new apartment. She really like it, especially her new bookshelves. But they needed something pretty, to decorate them.

"What can I make to put on my shelves?" she asked her friend Jennifer.

"I know!" said Jen. "We have some salt and some food coloring. Let's find a pretty bottle and make a salt picture!"

"A salt picture!" exclaimed Claudia. "What is that?!"

Jennifer used this recipe to show Claudia what to do, and Claudia had a lot of fun layering the salt into the bottle and making mountains and valleys. When she finished, she had a beautiful salt picture to put on her shelf!

**Colored Salt**
3 cups salt
2 tbs liquid tempura or food coloring

Mix  the salt and the coloring or tempura and
let it dry. Use just like colored sand.

Claudia could have made her picture with
sand, too. To find out how, and some other
artful things to do with rice, pasta, and  other
stuff in the kitchen, see the back of the book.
And then, check the back of the book for some
other fun stuff that didn't fit anywhere else!

Have fun making and playing with your craft
supplies!

# 1. MOLDING AND SCULPTING

## Play Dough

1 C. flour 1/2 C. salt
2 tsp. cream of tartar 2 tsp. oil
1 C. water
1 tsp. cinnamon
Food coloring

Mix ingredients in a saucepan; cook 3 minutes on high, or until dough begins to pull away from the side of the pan and forms a ball. Place dough on counter to cool; knead cinnamon and food coloring into dough. Divide dough and place into airtight container.

## Play Clay

2 cups Baking Soda
1 Cup Corn Starch
1 1/4 cup water

Cook over med heat, stirring constantly till texture of mashed potatoes. Cool, then knead well. Pat or roll out; cut with cookie cutter to desired shapes.

Finished item may be air dried for several days or bake at 175 degrees for about 40 minutes. Decorate as desired.

**Handprint Dough**

2 cups of flour
1 cup salt
1 cup water
Food coloring
Ribbon
Wax paper
Markers

Add food coloring to the water. Mix all ingredients well, kneading until smooth. Dough should not be soft or runny or it will fill with air bubbles when baking.
Form dough into a smooth ball. Using a rolling pin with the dough on wax paper, roll out as round as you can. Dough will be about 1/2 inch thick.
Press your child's hand with fingers splayed into the dough. Press deeply but don't touch the bottom. (When it bakes it tends to raise the handprint up.)
Put on a cookie sheet. Poke two holes in the top about 1/2 inch apart.
Bake at 200 degrees for about 2-3 hours. Dough should be fairly hard
When they are done and cooled, use markers to decorate as desired. Thread a ribbon

through the holes at the top to use as a loop to hang.

## Edible Play Dough

1 cup peanut butter
1 cup honey
2 cups powdered milk

This dough is naturally yummy!
Mix all the ingredients in a bowl. Knead until smooth with your clean hands.
Form the dough into shapes and then eat them for a snack.

## Bread Sculpting Dough

2 pieces of bread
1/4 bottle of white glue (4 oz. bottle)
Food coloring

Crumble bread into small chunks.
Add glue. Mix immediately. If too dry or sticky add a little water.
Work like clay, but don't crumble or handle for too long. Sculptures will dry in about an hour, usually.
When dry, you can spray with hair spray or paint with clear nail polish for shine and endurance.

## Candy Clay

1/3 c Margarine
1/3 c Light corn syrup
1/4 ts Salt
1 ts Vanilla or Peppermint
1 lb Powdered Sugar

Mix the first 4 ingredients. Add sugar, knead.

## Coffee Grounds Dough

2 c Used, dry coffee grounds
1/2 c Salt
1 1/2 c Cornmeal
Warm water

Mix dry ingredients together. Add enough warm water to moisten.
This dough has a unusual texture and is good for patting, rolling, and pounding.

## Dryer Lint Clay

1 1/2 c Lint from the dryer
1 c Water
1/2 c Regular flour
Old newspaper
Paint

Cover lint with water in a saucepan. When thoroughly wet, add the flour and stir until it is smooth.

Cook the mixture, stirring constantly, until it forms peaks and holds together.

Pour it onto newspaper to cool.

Use it like clay, or cover a balloon or other form with it.

Allow to dry for 3 to 5 days, then paint and decorate as desired.

## Edible Oatmeal Fun Dough

2 c Uncooked oatmeal
1 c Flour
1/4 c Water

Mix and knead. It doesn't taste good, but it's harmless if swallowed.

## Edible Peanut Butter and Syrup Fun Dough

1 c Peanut butter
1 c Corn syrup
1 1/2 c Powdered sugar
1 1/2 c Powdered milk

Mix all ingredients together with a spoon. Add more powdered milk if necessary to make a workable dough. Knead, shape, and eat.

## Fun Dough - Definitely Edible

1/4 c Brown Sugar
1/4 c Peanut Butter
1 tb Granola

Mix. Play. Eat.

## Powdered Drink Play Dough

2 pkg Non-sweetened powdered drink
2 c Flour
1/2 c Salt
2 ts Alum
2 c Water; boiled
3 tb Oil

Mix the drink powder, flour, salt and alum together. Add the water and oil. Knead. Add more flour if needed to reduce stickiness. This smells great.

## Decorated Dough Jars

4 cups flour
1 cup salt
1 cup hot water
Plastic jars with lids
Glitter
Glue
sequins, rhinestones, etc.

Mix flour, salt, and hot water.
Mix and knead well.
Mold dough onto the jar lids.   Let it air dry.
Decorate with glitter, sequins, rhinestones, or
whatever you like.  (Glue to dough)

## Sand Sculpture

2 c Sand
1 c Cornstarch
1 c Water a spoon

Mix the sand, cornstarch, and water together in
a saucepan. Heat the mixture over low heat
and keep stirring; remove from heat when the
mixture is thick. Let the mixture cool, then
make your sculpture. Allow sculpture to dry
and harden.

## Sawdust and Flour Molding Mixture

4 c Sawdust (strained)
2 c Flour
1 c Water
2 tb White liquid glue

Mix sawdust and flour. Gradually add water
until the dough holds together. Before forming
objects for drying and painting, add 2
tablespoons of white liquid glue.
Chocolate Scented Play Dough

flour
cocoa powder
salt
cream of tartar
cooking oil
boiling water

Mix 1 1/4 cups of flour, 1/2 cup cocoa
powder, 1/2 cup salt,1/2 Tablespoon cream of
tartar. Add 1 1/2 Tablespoons cooking oil, 1
cup boiling water.
Stir quickly, mix well. Cook over low heat until
dough forms a ball. When cool, mix with your
hands. Store in airtight container. Smells great
and is harmless if swallowed but does not taste
good so kids won't eat it up.

## Clean Mud

warm water (warm enough to melt soap)
1 bar dove soap
1 roll white toilet paper

Let children tear the toilet paper into very
small pieces. With a hand grater, grate the bar
of soap into a big bowl. Add the torn up toilet
paper to the bowl. Add the warm water a little
bit at a time while mixing the toilet paper and
the soap together to the consistency of
whipped cream. The mixture gets fluffier as it
is handled. Kids love it!

## Spice Dough - Edible

2 c Flour
2 ts Baking Powder
1/3 c Sugar
1/2 ts Salt
1/2 ts Cinnamon
1/4 ts Nutmeg
1/3 c Water
4 tb Salad Oil

Mix dry ingredients. Add water and oil. Knead until dough sticks and forms a ball.

As long as children use clean hands on clean surfaces and nothing gets dropped, this mixture can be fried in oil and eaten after play.

## 2. PAINTING AND COLORING

### Puffy Paint

Flour
Salt
Water
Tempera Paint
Mix  flour, salt and water. Add liquid tempera
paint in the desired color. Pour into squeeze
bottles. When squeezed
onto paper, the paint will harden into puffy
shapes.

### Poster Paint

1 tsp Vinegar
1 tsp. cornstarch
20 drops of desired Food Coloring

Mix vinegar, cornstarch, and coloring in baby
food
jar and shake to mix.

### Crayon Soap

1 cup grated ivory soap
1/4 cup warm water
food coloring
ice trays or cookie cutters

1. Mix water, soap, and food coloring together
in a medium bowl. Stir

until it begins to stiffen.
2. Remove the mixture from the bowl and
knead until it is the consistency
of a very thick dough.
3. Spoon into ice trays or cookie cutters.
4. Place in the freezer for 10 minutes.
5. Pop the crayons out and allow the to dry
overnight or until hard.

**Face Paint**

1 tsp. Cornstarch
1/2 tsp. Cold cream
1/2 tsp. Cold water
Food coloring

Mix together all ingredients. Use different food
colorings to create different colors, and paint
away. This comes right off with cold cream.

## Body Paint

2 cups baby shampoo
powdered tempura paint

Mix paint with shampoo to desired color. This
comes off easily with water.

## Condensed Milk Paint

1 c Condensed milk
Food coloring

Mix one cup condensed milk with a few drops
of food coloring. This makes a very bright,
glossy paint.

## Cornstarch Finger Paint

3 tb Sugar
1/2 c Cornstarch
2 c Cold water
Food coloring
Soap flakes

Cook sugar and cornstarch in medium
saucepan over low heat. Add cold water and
stir until mixture is thick. Remove from heat.
Divide into four or five portions. Add a drop
or two of food coloring to each portion and a

pinch of soap flakes. Stir and let cool. Store in airtight container.

## Pudding Paint

For young children, prepare instant chocolate pudding and let them do creative finger painting with no danger if some finds its way to their mouths!

## Edible Finger Paints

Baby rice cereal
food coloring

Mix rice cereal with water and food coloring. Paint.

## Eggshell Sidewalk Chalk

6 Eggshells
1 ts Very hot water from the tap
1 ts Flour

Wash eggshells so they are clean and egg-free. Dry them well. Take them outside and grind them with a clean rock on the sidewalk or other clean concrete surface.  Don't get dirt ground in with the eggshells. Grind the eggshells into a fine powder. You'll need one soup spoonful of this powder to make a stick

of chalk. Children have a lot of energy for
grinding; I suggest you make use of them.
When you have enough powder, pick out any
little bits of eggshell that are still not ground
up and throw them away. Scoop the eggshell
powder into a paper towel and bring it inside.
Measure the flour and the hot water into a
small dish. Stir them together to make a paste.
Put a soup spoonful of eggshell powder into
the paste and mix well. You may need to mash
it with the back of the spoon.

Shape this mixture into a chalk stick. Then roll
it up in a strip of paper towel. Let it dry.
Drying takes about three days. After three days
it's ready to use. Just peel the paper off one
end and you're ready for some sidewalk art.

(This chalk is for the sidewalks only, not for
chalkboards.)

### Homemade Paint

1 ts Vinegar
1 ts Cornstarch
20 dr Food coloring

Put all ingredients in a small jar and shake
until mixed. If too thin, add more cornstarch; if
too thick, add more vinegar.

## Invisible Ink

Lemon juice

Quick and easy... just use a toothpick or fine brush to 'write' your secret message on a piece of paper. To make the message appear, hold the paper over a lightbulb or flashlight.

## Paint With Butter

Melted butter or margarine
Food coloring
Bread
Paint brush

Mix desired color of food coloring with melted butter or margarine. Give child an unused paint brush and a slice of bread. Have them paint the bread, using several different colors, if desired. Then put bread in toaster until brown.

## Sidewalk Chalk

1 c Plaster of paris
1/2 c Cool water
Poster paints

Mix all ingredients together in a bowl and then pour into paper baking cups. When dried, peel off the paper.

## Giant Crayons

1 ounce paraffin or candle wax
3 tablespoon powdered tempura
paper towel tubes

Melt wax over the stove in a old pot. Add the paint pigment. Put as many paper towel tubes in a coffee can as will fit so they won't fall over. Carefully pour the mixture into the paper towel tubes. When the wax is dry, peel away the paper towel tubes> These are GREAT fun!

## Glitter Paint

1/4 cup hot water (not boiling)
3 teaspoon epsom salts

Mix. Paint on darker colored paper. When dry, paint will glitter.

## Face Makeup

Nonfat powdered milk
Water
Food coloring

Mix powdered milk and water so that mixture is thick.  Add food coloring.

**Whipped Cream Art**

Whipped cream
food coloring
heavy paper

Mix whipped cream and a little food coloring together, stirring lightly. This will dry like 3D paint. Makes great finger paint.

**Powdered Gelatin Paint**

Any powdered gelatin mixed with a little boiling water to the right consistency makes great smelling, safe finger paint.

**Snowy Day Paint**

food coloring
water
spray bottles

Mix food coloring and water in spray bottles and let the children spray paint the snow!

**Face or Body Paint**
¼ c Baby lotion
small amount Liquid detergent
Powdered tempera paint

Mix the ingredients together, adding paint to desired color. Washs off easily.

## Painting With Pasta

Cook some linguine or spaghetti and let it cool. Pour several colors of food coloring into bowls. Let the kids mix the pasta with the food coloring: this is good, squishy fun. Give the kids pieces of heavy paper (like construction or poster paper) and let them use the pasta to paint on it. The pasta will be perfectly safe if your little artists decide to eat it.

## 3. STICKY STUFF

### Classroom Paste

1 cup non-self-rising wheat flour
1 cup sugar
1 cup cold water
4 cups boiling water
1 tbls. powdered alum
1/2 tsp. oil of cinnamon (optional)

Combine flour and sugar in a large pot. Slowly
stir in cold water to form a paste.
Slowly add boiling water, stirring vigorously
to break up lumps.
Bring mixture to a boil, stirring constantly,
until thick and clear.
Remove from heat and add alum. Stir until
well mixed.
Add oil of cinnamon if paste will not be used
immediately.
Makes 1 1/2 quarts.

### Decoupage Glue

3 part white glue
1 part warm water

Combine glue with water in a jar. Shake til
well-mixed.

## Waterproof or Glass Glue

2 packets (1/2 ounce) unflavored gelatin
2 tbsp. cold water
3 tbsp. skim milk

In a small bowl, sprinkle gelatin over cold water. Set aside to soften.
 Heat milk to boiling point and pour into softened gelatin. Stir until gelatin is dissolved.

NOTE: Oil of cloves can be added as a preservative if this is not to be used at once.

## Papier Mache' Paste

3 C. water
1 1/2 C. flour
Oil of peppermint (optional)

Stir flour into cold water.  Cook over low heat until the
mixture thickens to a creamy paste.  Add more water if the paste gets too thick. Cool.  Add a few drops of peppermint oil for scent.  Use the paste to coat paper strips.

## 4. GOOD OL' GOO

### Flubber

Metamucil
Water

Place a teaspoon of Metamucil in a jar with 8-10 ounces of water.
Shake vigorously for about 60 seconds
Pour contents into a medium cereal bowl.
Place the bowl in microwave at full power for 4-5 minutes It will start to " rise" just like bread dough...but in fast speed.
Turn off the microwave when bubbles are just about to overflow the bowl
 Let it cool slightly and repeat- the more often you repeat this the more rubbery flubber will become (five times should do it )
Pour onto a plate or cookie sheet. Keep children away at this point! Teacher should stir until it cools.  . When finished it's cool and clammy but not sticky. Flubber will last for several months if tightly sealed or refrigerated.

## Silly Putty

2 parts white glue
1 part liquid starch

Mix ingredients and let dry to a workable
consistency. Add more glue or starch if
necessary.  Store in an airtight container.

## Gooey Gunk

1 1/3 cup warm water
4 tsp. borax laundry booster

1 cup water
1 cup white glue
7-10 drops of food coloring

Mix water, glue and food coloring in a medium
sized bowl. In another bowl, mix the water and
borax til the borax is dissolved. Slowly pour
the borax mix into the glue mix. Roll it around
4 or 5 times. Lift the borax mix out and knead
it for 2 or 3 minutes. Store in a air=tight
container.

## 5. BUBBLE STUFF

### Crazy Bubbles

Put 1 quart of water in a shallow tub. Stir in 1/2 cup sugar until it
dissolves. Add 1/2 cup dishwashing liquid &stir again. Have kids dip in
a slotted kitchen spoon or fly swatter, & swing it in the air. You can
also cut both ends out of an empty frozen juice can. Dip one end in the
bubbles &blow through the other. Makes huge bubbles!
Note: For color, add food coloring. You can also buy glycerin at the drug store and add a few tablespoons to make bubbles last longer.

### Bubble Blower

1 Drinking straw
1 six pack plastic holder (from cans)
Bowl or pan (to pour bubbles into)

Tape the holder to the straw. Dip into bubbles and swirl around.

Add food coloring for color. (optional)

## Bubble Stuff 2

1/3 c Dish soap or baby shampoo
1 1/4 c Water
2 tsp Sugar
Food coloring

Combine ingredients and pour into an
unbreakable bottle.

## Bubble Stuff 3

6 c Water
2 c Crystal Octagon dishwashing liquid
3/4 c Light corn syrup

Mix all the ingredients together in a dishpan.
Pour into a bottle.

## 6. HOLIDAY CRAFTS

### Parade Streamers

Use an empty paper towel roll. Cover it with construction paper.  Decorate with glitter, paint, or caryons. Now tape or glue colorful crepe paper or construction paper strips  to one end. You're ready to have a parade!

### For Mother's Day:

### Button Flowers

What you need: Stiff construction paper or Oak Tag
Scissors
Pipe cleaners
Buttons

Cut out flowers from different colors of construction paper.
Center a button with the middle of your flower. Poke a pipe cleaner through your flower so that it comes up and through the first hole of your button, then poke it down through the next hole in the button and through your flower.
Twist the short end of the pipe cleaner around the long end, directly under the flower and button.

**For Halloween:**

**Bubbling Magic Cauldron**

Cauldron
Water
Baking soda
Vinegar
Tablespoon
Cup
Pan or tray

Place a cauldron on a pan or tray (cauldrons are abundant around Halloween.) Place 2 tbsp. of water in the cauldron and stir in 1 tbsp. of baking soda. In a separate cup, measure 2 tbsp. of vinegar. Pour it in and watch potion bubble! You can explain that this happens because vinegar is an acid and baking soda is a base and when they combine, it forms carbon dioxide, for a little science fun.

**For Christmas:**

**Cinnamon Scented Decorations**

1 cup cinnamon
1 tsp crushed cloves
1 tsp nutmeg
3/4 cup applesauce
2 tbsp white glue

Mix all together until smooth. Cut with cookie cutters or mold into shapes to 1/4" or 1/2" thick. Use a regular drinking straw to poke holes in top for hanging cord.
Dry at room temperature;  add glitter, paint or decorate as desired.

**Play Craft Snow**

Ivory Snow (powder form)
Water
Electric mixer
Mixing bowl

Mix water and Ivory Snow on high til it forms peaks like meringue. Use it to paint on cardboard. When dry, it looks like snow.

**Magic Reindeer Food**

Mix together oatmeal and glitter. Put some of the mixture in a
small plastic bag.

On a heavy piece of paper.  print the following instructions.

MAGIC REINDEER FOOD

On Christmas Eve, sprinkle the Magic Reindeer Food around your yard--The glitter sparkling in the moonlight and the smell of the oats will lead Rudolph to your house.

Fold the paper rectangle in half and staple to the top of the bag.

# 7. MISCELLANEOUS CRAFT ITEMS

## Colored Sand

3 cups clean sand (check the aquarium section of pet stores)
2 tbs. liquid tempura

Mix the ingredients and allow to dry, stirring occasionally. It will take about 24 hours to dry. For deeper colors, use more paint.

## Colored Salt

3 cups salt
2 tbs liquid tempura or food coloring

Mix and let dry. Use like colored sand.

## Colored Sand 2

1 c Sand
1/8 c Water (approximately)
Food coloring

Mix food coloring with water, stir in sand, spread out and let dry a couple of hours.

**Macaroni Pictures**

Have various shapes of pasta to choose from.
Let children glue these onto colored paper for
creative pictures.

**Colored Rice**

1 cup white rice
1 tsp. rubbing alcohol
food coloring

Mix a few drops of food coloring with alcohol.
Put rice in sealable container. Pour liquid
mixture over rice and shake until color is
evenly distributed. Spread colored rice in a
thin layer to dry. Store rice in dry air-tight
container.

**Colored Pasta**

pasta shapes
food color
rubbing alcohol
plastic bag

Place pasta in plastic bag, add 6-8 drops of
food coloring and one tsp of rubbing alcohol
and shake. Pour onto cookie sheet to dry for
about 5-10 minutes.

## 8. A FEW GREAT THINGS THAT DIDN'T FIT

### Easy Potpourri

Rose petals (or petals from any other flower that smells really nice)
Salt
Whole cloves

Put the petals in a large bowl.
Sprinkle some salt on the petals and stir gently.
Sprinkle a handful of cloves and stir gently again.
Place in a pretty container and cover with clear plastic wrap.

This would make a great gift for Mother's Day, Christmas, etc.

### Crystal Gardens

6 tbsp Salt
6 tbsp Liquid bluing
6 tbsp Water
1 tbsp Ammonia

Combine salt, bluing, water and ammonia. Pour over small pieces of rock or coal in a shallow GLASS or CHINA bowl. Drip food coloring on top if desire. Crystals will begin to grow soon. Add water occasionally to keep crystals growing. You'll probably want to place dish on tray or wooden board as crystals grow over the sides of the bowl.


**Rock Candy**

1 Glass jar or drinking glass
1 Piece of cotton string
1 Pencil or stick
1 Paper clip
1 Food coloring (optional)
1 c Water
2 c Sugar
Additional sugar

Tie a  piece of string to the middle of the pencil or stick. Attach a paper clip to the end of the string for a weight. Moisten the string very lightly, and roll in a bit of sugar (this will "attract" the sugar crystals from the syrup to the string). Place the pencil or stick over the top of the glass or jar with the string hanging down inside.
Heat the water to boiling, and dissolve the 2 cups of sugar into it. For the biggest crystals fast, heat the sugar-water solution again, and dissolve as much additional sugar as you can into it. Add a few drops of food coloring to the solution if desired.

Pour the solution into the prepared glass or jar and leave undisturbed for a couple of days.

Depending on how much sugar you were able to dissolve into the water, you should start to see crystals growing in a few hours to a few days.

Rhetta Akamatsu is a freelance writer and the author of Ghost to Coast: A Paranormal Handbook. She is the grandmother of Claudia, William, and Sebastian. Although the stories in the book are fiction, the children are very real!

Rhetta maintains the website, Fabulous Freebies and Fun Links for Kids, at http://www.maxandstar.info, and has published a weekly ezine of that same name for over seven years. You can sign up for the free newsletter at http://www.yahoogroups.com/group/kids-freebies.

Rhetta lives in Marietta, GA, with her husband, Ken, and their two cats.

CPSIA information can be obtained at www.ICGtesting.com
Printed in the USA
LVOW121459020513

332035LV00017B/1007/P